Disney·PIXAR

WALL·E

Level 5

Re-told by: Louise Fonceca
Series Editor: Rachel Wilson

Contents

In This Book   iii

Before You Read   iv

Chapter 1: The Last Robot on Earth   1

Chapter 2: WALL-E Meets EVE   5

Chapter 3: EVE and the Plant   7

Chapter 4: Off to the Axiom   12

Chapter 5: Looking for the Plant   18

Chapter 6: The Captain Helps   23

After You Read   29

Glossary   30

Play: Life on Earth   32

Global Citizenship: Protect the Planet to Help People   33

Find Out: What's in our solar system?   34

Phonics   36

In This Book

WALL-E

The last robot on Earth. His job is to find trash

EVE

A white robot from the Axiom who meets WALL-E

The Axiom

A space station where people from Earth live

M-O

A small robot on the Axiom. His job is to clean things

The Captain

The most important person on the Axiom

Auto

A robot who is the Axiom's pilot

Before You Read

Introduction

WALL-E is a robot who lives on Earth and finds trash. He's the only thing that lives on Earth. One day he meets EVE, another robot. WALL-E and EVE become friends. WALL-E gives EVE a plant that he found. Suddenly, a spaceship takes EVE away, but WALL-E holds on to the spaceship and goes with her. They land on the Axiom, where all the people from Earth now live. The captain of the Axiom sees the plant and is very excited.

. . . .

Activities

1 **Read the *Introduction* and look at the picture on page 1. Answer the questions.**

1 What does WALL-E look like?

2 How do you think he feels?

3 What do you think his life is like?

2 **Now look at the other pictures in the story. Find these things in the story. Write the page numbers in your notebook.**

1 Some cubes of trash

2 A robot dancing

3 A robot holding the outside of a spaceship

4 Two people sitting on chairs

The Last Robot on Earth

A little robot called WALL-E moved through the mountains of trash on planet Earth.

The people escaped a long time ago when Earth became too dirty and dangerous. They all went to live on a big space station and left behind a lot of robots to clean the planet. Now, WALL-E was the only robot on Earth.

Soon, WALL-E arrived at his home—an old truck. *Whoosh!* He heard the sound of a storm and he closed the door quickly.

WALL-E's home had pretty lights and shelves full of interesting
things. He took out some things which he found in the trash that
day. He put them carefully on the shelves. Then he watched his
favorite movie. A man and a woman danced and held hands in the
movie. WALL-E loved it and he watched it again and again.

He wanted to hold hands and dance like the people in the
movie. But more than anything, he wanted a friend.

The next day, WALL-E went out to work. Every day, he put trash into his chest and squashed it to make neat cubes.

He often found interesting things in the trash. This time he found a big, red fire extinguisher. *Whoosh!* The fire extinguisher was fun!

Then he saw an old fridge … Behind the door he found something small and green. He really liked the green thing. He put it carefully into an old boot.

Just then, WALL-E saw a strange red light at his feet. The light raced away and he ran after it. Then he saw a lot more red lights …

Suddenly, there was a loud noise above him and WALL-E looked up. The lights were from a big spaceship. It nearly landed on WALL-E!

A big metal arm came out of the spaceship. The arm put something on the ground—it was white and round.

2 WALL-E Meets EVE

The spaceship took off and WALL-E hid behind a rock.

The white thing started to fly around like a bird. Sometimes it stopped and scanned things with a blue light. It flew near to WALL-E. Now he could see what it was—a female robot with big blue eyes. She was very beautiful.

He moved to hide behind another rock, but he made a noise. The robot turned and shot the rock with her arm.

WALL-E was scared, but he was okay. The white robot saw him at last. She flew toward him and scanned him with her blue light.

A little later she asked, "Name?"

At first, WALL-E didn't understand, but then he answered, "Wwwaaallee!"

The white robot then said her name, "EVE."

"Eeevaah? Eee-vah! Eevah!" said WALL-E. EVE laughed.

Suddenly, WALL-E heard the wind. It was another storm. WALL-E took EVE to his truck.

EVE and the Plant

WALL-E showed EVE a lot of things in his truck. Then he showed her his favorite movie. She watched the people singing and dancing. WALL-E copied the dancing for EVE. He turned around and around. EVE tried to dance, too. She turned very fast and hit WALL-E! *SMASH!*

She broke one of his eyes. Everything was okay because WALL-E found a new eye on one of his shelves.

EVE picked up one of WALL-E's things from the shelves.
She held it up and WALL-E moved closer. She looked so beautiful.
WALL-E wanted to hold her hand, but he was too shy.

He wanted to find something interesting for EVE. Then he
suddenly remembered the small green thing! He held up the boot
with the green thing inside. EVE looked very surprised to see a plant!
Then something very strange happened …

First, EVE scanned the plant with her blue light. Then two doors in her chest opened and the light pulled the plant inside. *Whoosh!*

Next, her arms and head closed into her body. A green light shone from her chest.

"Eevah!" WALL-E shouted, but she couldn't hear him. "Eevah!" he called again, but EVE couldn't move. What could WALL-E do to help his new friend?

WALL-E tried a lot of different things to wake her up. He took her for long walks. He sat with her for hours. Nothing worked.

The next day, WALL-E had to leave EVE and go to work. He just did his job and nothing more. He didn't look for things in the trash. He could only think about EVE.

Suddenly, he heard a loud noise and saw a red light in the sky. Was it another storm?

No, it wasn't a storm—it was the big spaceship. A robot arm came out of the spaceship and picked up EVE. WALL-E raced toward the spaceship.

"Eevah! Eevah!" he cried, but he was too late.

Then, the doors closed and WALL-E jumped onto the side of the spaceship. The spaceship took off and WALL-E held on with his small, metal hands.

4 Off to the Axiom

The spaceship flew by the moon, stars, and planets. Earth didn't look so ugly from space.

Soon, he saw something big and white in front of him. It was the Axiom—the space station where the people from Earth now lived.

The spaceship landed on the Axiom. The doors opened and WALL-E saw some white robots with EVE. She was the only one with a green light.

A robot arm picked up EVE and put her on the Axiom. WALL-E
sat with the other white robots and the arm picked him up, too.

Some little robots arrived. They cleaned the robots from the ship.
A little robot called M-O tried to clean WALL-E. He looked very dirty!

A smaller robot called Gopher arrived. He was the Captain's
robot. He scanned all the white robots. When he scanned EVE,
an alarm started—it made a terrible noise!

Gopher took Eve and drove her away quickly. WALL-E raced after them and M-O ran behind—he still wanted to clean WALL-E!

Soon, they arrived on the deck of the Axiom. There were people everywhere, but they didn't look like the people in WALL-E's favorite movie —they were much larger, softer, and rounder. They couldn't walk so they went everywhere in chairs. They all had TV screens in front of their faces. They looked very bored.

Gopher and EVE arrived outside the Captain's room. The doors opened and Gopher drove inside. WALL-E followed them, then he hid in a corner.

In the center of the room was a big wheel. It was a robot called Auto and he was the Axiom's pilot. He was there to help the Captain, but he decided everything.

Auto scanned EVE. A picture of a plant appeared on his computer screen. He had to call the Captain.

The Captain arrived. He looked at EVE and saw the picture of the plant on the computer screen. He pushed a big green button and a man appeared on the screen.

"Hello, Captain!" the man said. "I have fantastic news. If a plant can grow on Earth, people can live there, too. You can all go home! Just put the plant in the detector. The Axiom will take you home in no time!"

The Captain was excited. He wanted to see the plant and put it in the detector. The doors in EVE's chest opened, but there was no plant inside! WALL-E came out and looked everywhere for the plant.

Auto scanned EVE again, but he couldn't find anything. "This robot is broken," he told the Captain.

"Send her to the robot hospital," said the Captain. Then he pointed at WALL-E. "And clean this robot!"

 5 Looking for the Plant

WALL-E and EVE arrived at the robot hospital. It was full of sick and broken robots. A small pink robot jumped in front of WALL-E and painted his face. She held up a mirror. "Oh! You look so pretty!" she said.

They put WALL-E in a room next to a very sick robot. Then they put EVE in another room. They held her down and took off her arm. WALL-E saw everything through the glass walls. He had to save her!

CRASH! WALL-E broke through the glass and went into EVE's room. He picked up her arm and shot into the air.

Seconds later, a lot of broken robots raced into the room. They picked up WALL-E and carried him out of the hospital. EVE flew after them …

Suddenly, some police robots arrived. EVE flew down and picked up WALL-E and her arm. The broken robots stopped the police robots so EVE and WALL-E could escape!

EVE took WALL-E to a little rocket on the side of the Axiom. She wanted to save her friend. She pointed at the rocket and said, "Earth."

WALL-E went in and sat down. He pointed at the seat next to him. "Eevah?" he said softly. EVE pointed at the green light in her chest. She had to stay and find the plant.

WALL-E raced out of the rocket. He didn't want to go anywhere without EVE.

Just then, they heard a noise … It was Gopher!

WALL-E and EVE hid in the dark outside the little rocket.
Gopher opened the doors in his chest and took out … the plant!
He put it in the rocket and came out. EVE was very surprised,
but now she understood. It was Gopher who stole the plant!

She turned to WALL-E, but he wasn't there. He was in the rocket.
He went to get the plant!

"WALL-E!" EVE shouted, but it was too late. Gopher pushed a button and the rocket took off with WALL-E and the plant! EVE quickly took off, too. She had to follow WALL-E.

WALL-E was scared. He pushed a lot of buttons. Then he pushed the wrong button. "This rocket will explode in ten seconds," said a robot voice.

KA-BOOM! The rocket exploded and threw WALL-E into space. EVE flew toward WALL-E and caught him in her arms.

6 **The Captain Helps**

WALL-E and EVE danced together in space. Then WALL-E opened the door in his chest and showed the plant to EVE. She was so happy, she gave WALL-E a robot kiss!

Soon they were back on the Axiom. EVE wanted to take the plant to the Captain. She showed WALL-E a trash chute. It went up to the Captain's room.

EVE went into the chute and WALL-E waited for her.

EVE flew up the chute and took the plant to the Captain.
He was surprised but very happy. "Turn on the plant detector!"
he told Auto. "We're going home!"

"NO!" Auto shouted. "We are staying here! Give me the plant!"

"NO!" answered the Captain. "I am the Captain and we are
going home today!"

Suddenly, Gopher raced into the room. He took the plant and
threw it into the trash chute. Then he threw EVE into the chute, too!

WALL-E went to find EVE. He climbed up the chute ...

He caught the plant, but he couldn't catch EVE. They fell down the chute and landed in a mountain of trash. Some big robots picked up the trash and squashed it into cubes. WALL-E and EVE were in the cubes!

Quickly, EVE shot through the cube and escaped. Then she pulled WALL-E from his cube. He was badly broken, but he still had the plant!

In the Captain's room, Auto still didn't want to turn on the detector. He didn't want anything to change. He didn't want to go back to Earth!

The Captain had an idea. Secretly, he turned on the computer and started to talk. His face appeared on every screen on the Axiom.

"EVE … the detector is near the swimming pool. Put the plant inside!" Then, for the first time in his life, he stood up and walked toward Auto …

The Captain fought bravely with Auto and won! He pushed the robot away and turned on the detector.

EVE flew with WALL-E to the swimming pool and put the plant in the detector. Ten, nine, eight, seven, six ... *Whoosh!*

The Axiom landed on Earth and the doors opened. The Captain and all the people looked at their true home. They stood up and walked slowly out of the Axiom to their new life.

EVE flew with WALL-E to his truck and changed his broken parts.

WALL-E looked at EVE with his new eyes. At first, he couldn't remember her. But then she gave him a kiss and he remembered! "Eevah!" he said softly.

EVE held WALL-E's hand and looked into his eyes. She loved him and he loved her. At last, WALL-E had everything he ever wanted.

Global Citizenship

Protect the Planet to Help People

Autumn Peltier is a teenager but she's already changing the world.

This schoolgirl lives near a large lake in Ontario, Canada. One day, she found out that many people near her didn't have clean water to drink. She became very angry about this. She believes that all people need clean water. So, she decided to do something about it.

Autumn talked to a lot of important people about the problem and they promised to help. Now, because of her, more people in Canada have clean water. Today, Autumn still works to get clean water for all.

In 2019, Autumn spoke at the Global Landscapes Forum in New York. "We can't eat money or drink oil," she said.

What's in our solar system?

In our solar system, there's the Sun, eight planets, and many moons. Everything in the solar system moves around the Sun.

The International Space Station (ISS)

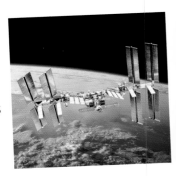

It takes 90 minutes for the ISS to go around the Earth—that's 16 times a day! The ISS is as big as a soccer field, and six people can live on it at the same time. Astronauts from different countries stay on the ISS to study space.

Space Trash

Trash is everywhere—and not just on Earth. There are millions of pieces of trash in space, too.

Space trash is anything that astronauts leave behind. It can be small pieces of metal or large, old rockets. Space trash is a big problem because it travels very fast. It can hit spaceships or the ISS and this is dangerous.

All the countries that go into space must try to find an answer to this problem.

Did you know?

- The Sun is a star, not a planet.
- Scientists think our solar system is 4.6 billion years old.
- Venus is the hottest planet.
- Jupiter is the biggest planet.
- At night, you can sometimes see the International Space Station from Earth.

astronaut (*noun*) a person who works in space
million (*number*) 1,000,000 / one thousand thousand
billion (*number*) 1,000,000,000 / one thousand million

Phonics

Say the sounds. Read the words.

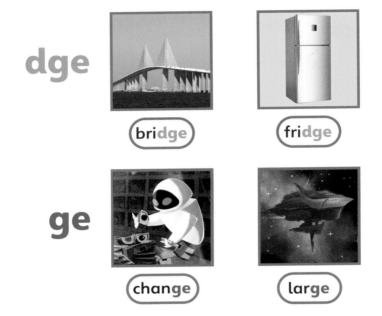

dge

bridge

fridge

ge

change

large

Read, then say the poem to a friend.

The large captain
Looks in the fridge.
He's feeling very hungry.

He sees a change.
No food? That's strange!
And now he's feeling angry.